Those Pe

humorous drawings by

Jeff Foxworthy

LONGSTREET PRESS
Atlanta, Georgia

Published by LONGSTREET PRESS, INC.,
a subsidiary of Cox Newspapers,
a subsidiary of Cox Enterprises, Inc.
2140 Newmarket Parkway
Suite 118
Marietta, Georgia 30067

Printed in the United States of America

1st printing, 1996

Library of Congress Catalog Number 95-82229

ISBN: 1-56352-297-7

This book was printed by Quebecor Printing/TN

Cover design by Jill Dible
Book design by Neil Hollingsworth
Cover photo by Steven Sigoloff

Digital film prep and separations by Advertising Technologies, Inc., Atlanta, GA

Jeff Foxworthy's award-winning humor is also available on two compact disks and audio tapes from Warner Bros. Records — "You Might Be a Redneck If..." and "Games Rednecks Play."

INTRODUCTION

Living on the road. A lot of people do it — salesmen, truckers, athletes, musicians, and yeah, even comedians. I've accumulated enough frequent flyer miles to circle the globe, yet all I want is a free ticket to sit on my couch in my underwear and eat a home-cooked meal. Sleeping in my own bed has become a treat, for many reasons, not the least of which is that my wife is there.

Not that living on the road is all bad. It certainly beats *dying* on the road. Just ask any possum. Doing sold-out shows is still a thrill and I find I still love being on stage. But that is only two hours of my day. The rest of it is spent mainly in airports, airplanes, and hotel rooms. It makes for lots of idle time . . . that thing your grandmother warned you about.

There are many ways to pass this time. You can read, you can sleep, or you can just sit back and watch people. I do a lot of the third one. I have always drawn to entertain myself, and sometimes these two activities come together. I am fascinated by the diversity of people, so when I see an interesting face or character, whether they be in a newspaper, magazine, or in line at a yogurt stand, I log it. Sometimes they show up in my stand-up routines, sometimes in my sketch book.

I depend on the stand-up routines to pay my bills, but the sketch book was just for my own enjoyment. I would show them to my wife, family members and friends. I never really planned on doing anything else with them until one day when my editor, Chuck Perry, and I were having lunch, my sketch book was in with some other stuff I was showing him. He looked through it, being careful not to smear the pages with barbecue sauce, and he laughed out loud. "Fox, this is a book," he said. I was surprised, but as my life has proven, stranger things have happened.

So here it is — **THOSE PEOPLE**. A collection of characters that you might live with, next door to, or have even seen along the way. If one should even happen to resemble you, I apologize. I've never had a formal art lesson.

Keep laughing,

Jeff Foxworthy

DEDICATION

For Jules, sunshine in shoes. I love you.

OTHER BOOKS BY JEFF FOXWORTHY

You Might Be A Redneck If...
Hick Is Chic
Red Ain't Dead
Check Your Neck
You're Not a Kid Anymore
Games Rednecks Play
Redneck Classic
No Shirt, No Shoes, No Problem

Those People

humorous drawings by

Jeff Foxworthy

Those People

THE GOOD LOOKS WERE DISTRIBUTED EQUALLY BETWEEN THE CRAWFORD SISTERS

IT WAS AFTER MIDNIGHT AND EDDIE
STILL WASN'T HOME

RON'S SEARCH TOOK HIM DOOR TO DOOR

SID SITS ON AN AIR JET

Those People

A SPONGE BATH TO REMEMBER

 already placed.

5

TRYING TO DECIDE IF THE MARE IS IN HEAT

THREE GLASSES OF WINE FOR MYRNA
AND THE OFFICE CHRISTMAS PARTY
WAS OFFICIALLY UNDER WAY

Those People

DON KING'S WIFE

"NO CROISSANTS!?"

FISHERMAN TED HOWARD SHOWS OFF A NICE BASS
AND HIS SON ZEKE

Those People

YES! LARRY DECIDED,
THIS REDLIGHT WAS FOLLOWING A PATTERN

Those People

IN THE WORLD OF BLANK STARES,
JOEY MUNERO WAS A PLAYER

AFTER WATCHING THE JENSENS TAKE A MIDGET AND A GOAT INSIDE, MARIE DECIDED TO CALL THE POLICE

Those People

CARL, THE VAMPIRE JANITOR

14

*EARL WISHED THE PUZZLES ON
"WHEEL OF FORTUNE" WERE NOT SO DIFFICULT*

WARREN ENJOYED SHARING HIS BELIEFS WITH OTHERS DURING THEIR LUNCH-HOUR

MISTAKING IT FOR A SNAKE, MANUEL KILLS HIS GARDEN HOSE

GERTRUDE LENDS HARRIET YET ANOTHER CUP OF SUGAR

Those People

PAUL KNEW YOU COULD SELL THEM A VACUUM
CLEANER IF YOU COULD HYPNOTIZE THEM

Those People

THE NEW BABY SITTER

20

THELMA WAS AMAZED THE COPS COULDN'T SEE THE LITTLE MEN IN HER OVEN

VIC TORIA'S SECRET

COUSIN JERRY WAS THE MAIN TOPIC OF CONVERSATION AT THE FAMILY REUNION

Those People

HURRY HOME, HONEY!

24

DOT PRACTICES FOR HER
DRIVER'S LICENSE PHOTO

IT WAS HARD TO KEEP A SECRET FROM CHARLOTTE

PAULINE AND MERV WAIT FOR HER PARENTS TO GO TO BED

CAROL FELT SHE WAS A PEACOCK IN A PREVIOUS LIFE

Those People

BAD NEWS FOR BREWSTER
...ANOTHER CAVITY

Those People

CLINT MOORE'S UNPATENTED HAND WARMER

Those People

410 PLUM STREET... AN ADDRESS PETE
THE POSTMAN WOULD NOT SOON FORGET

REVEREND WALKER EXPLAINS HOW THE DEVIL CREEPS INTO YOUR LIFE

PATTY WAITED FOR THE RIGHT MOMENT TO SPIT OUT THE CLAM DIP

THERE WAS SOMETHING ODD
ABOUT TED FROM THE MAIL ROOM

FAHAD DREADED ANOTHER SUMMER WITHOUT AIR-CONDITIONING

DARRELL WOULD SAY HE UNDERSTOOD,
BUT YOU GOT THE IMPRESSION HE DIDN'T

BUDDY WAS ABOUT TWO BEERS AWAY FROM
WHIPPING SOMEBODY'S ASS

MILDRED WILKENS
MECHANICAL BULL CHAMPION, SENIOR DIVISION

Those People

FOR JOEL, DISCO FEVER
WAS A TERMINAL DISEASE

40

KODAK MOMENT

TROY NOTICED THE GIRLS AT THE END OF THE BAR CHECKING HIM OUT

BANK MANAGER NATE DAVIS
INFORMS BUBBA HAYGOOD THAT HIS LOAN
HAS NOT BEEN APPROVED

GRANNY HAWKINS, CAT BURGLAR

Those People

CHARLIE BUYS A "GIRLIE" MAGAZINE

LONG BEFORE ANYONE ELSE COULD HEAR IT,
HELEN WOULD ANNOUNCE,
"THE ICE CREAM TRUCK IS COMING"

Those People

FURS, JEWELRY AND DEPENDS

48

POLICE HAVE A SUSPECT IN THE
FUDGE-SHOPPE ROBBERIES

WAITING TO BE DISCOVERED

Those People

LEON, TRANSMISSION SCHOOL VALEDICTORIAN

VERA'S WEDDING NIGHT

Those People

TROY DIDN'T HANG OUT WITH THE OTHER
8TH GRADERS DURING LUNCH

Those People

SHELDON'S GOLDFISH

54

Those People

INSURANCE SALESMAN NELSON FERRY
DEMONSTRATES THE PEACE OF MIND
THAT COMES WITH A WHOLE-LIFE POLICY

55

DAN TOLD A GREAT STORY
ABOUT HOW HE CAUGHT THE FISH, BUT
THE TRUTH WAS HE SIMPLY FOUND IT
IN HIS SWIMMING TRUNKS

Those People

THE SUMMER WASN'T COMPLETE UNTIL
TREY BAIRD'S MOTHER HAD BEEN BANNED
FROM THE LITTLE LEAGUE PARK

57

AFTER THE EGGNOG, AUNT FLORENCE STARTED GIVING EVERYONE "NOOGIES"

SURE, CARLENE HAD BEEN AROUND THE BLOCK
A FEW TIMES, BUT IT WAS A TRIP
SHE WAS STILL WILLING TO MAKE

*EDDIE AND WILLIE
A SPECIAL KIND OF LOVE STORY*

Those People

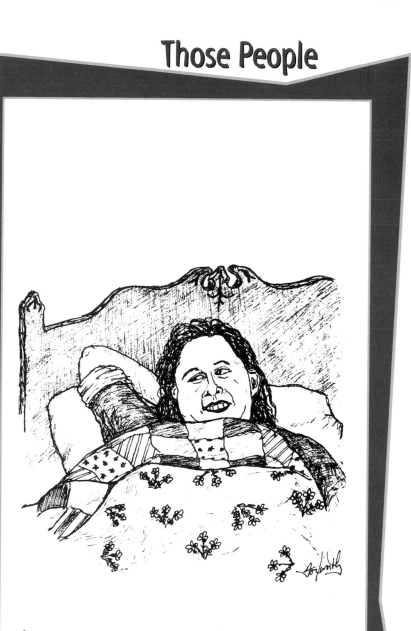

AFTER ALL THESE YEARS MARY STILL ENJOYED WATCHING EUGENE TAKE OFF HIS UNDERPANTS

MANNY SAT IN THE SHALLOWS AND WAITED TO DO
A LITTLE GIRL WATCHING

Those People

WAITING FOR THE JEHOVAH'S WITNESSES

Those People

*ONCE AGAIN DON PONDERED
THE AGE-OLD QUESTION — WHAT DO WOMEN WANT?*

64

Those People

$$X + Y = 2\frac{X^2}{Y \cdot 3}$$

$$X = 2\frac{X^2}{Y \cdot 3} - Y$$

$$X = \frac{X^2}{Y \cdot 3} - \frac{Y}{2}$$

MS. MOORE IS VOTED MOST POPULAR TEACHER AT EASTBROOK HIGH FOR THE SIXTH YEAR IN A ROW!

65

ARNOLD KNEW THE KEY TO FLY CATCHING WAS
PATIENCE, PATIENCE, PATIENCE

CHIN AND FU ENJOY A GOOD NINJA JOKE

BARBARA'S MOUSTACHE HAD ADVANCED TO THE STAGE THAT PEROXIDE COULD NO LONGER DISGUISE IT

WHAT JIM HAD HOPED WAS A CALL
FROM THE GOVERNOR ENDED UP BEING
SOMEONE SELLING TIME-SHARE CONDOS

DUANE "DRIFTS OFF" DURING
HIS PRO-MARIJUANA SPEECH

STILL FOUR MONTHS FROM HER DUE DATE,
PHYLISS WAS WORRIED ABOUT
THE BIRTHWEIGHT OF THIS BABY

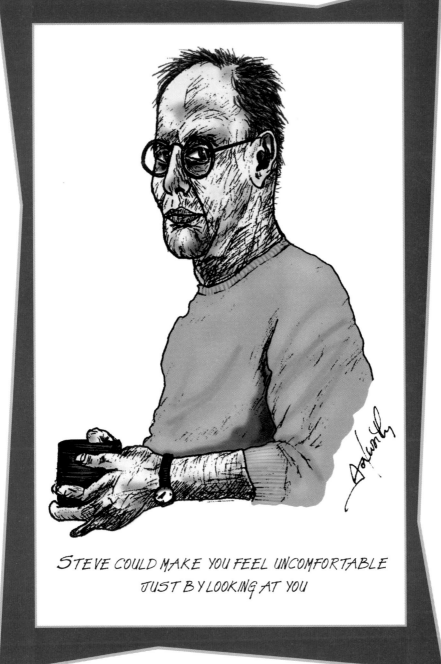

STEVE COULD MAKE YOU FEEL UNCOMFORTABLE JUST BY LOOKING AT YOU

Those People

JERRY'S NATIONAL TELEVISION DEBUT

Those People

*TED HAD A GIFT
HE FELT COMPELLED TO SHARE WITH OTHERS*

MURRAY CONFRONTS THE WALKERS ABOUT
THEIR PIT-BULL, WILLIE

TO SAVE THE COST OF AN EXTERMINATOR, EARL DECIDES TO TAKE CARE OF HIS MOUSE PROBLEM HIMSELF

Those People

CAP' AND ANGIE ANSWER THE AD
IN THE SWINGERS MAGAZINE

"THERE", THOUGHT MABEL, "THAT SHOULD KEEP CARL IN THE CLOSET FOR AWHILE"

I REMEMBER MAMA

WILLARD KNEW THAT WOMEN LIKED A MAN IN UNIFORM

BEDTIME STORIES

THINK! ROSA TOLD HERSELF...WHAT HAPPENED TO ALL OF THE FOOD?

MANY AT THE MORNING MEETING SUSPECTED NATE
HAD NOT MADE IT HOME LAST NIGHT

AUNT FRIEDA WOULD BE THE FIRST TO TELL YOU
SHE WAS NOT A PRETTY WOMAN WITHOUT HER WIG

Those People

"OH GOD," THOUGHT TINA, "WRONG PARTY"

SOME PEOPLE DENY THEIR SEXUALITY...
NOT DON WOODS

ROLLIE TOLD HIS MOTHER HE WAS GOING TO THE
MOVIES, BUT HE ALWAYS ENDED UP AT
THE KIT KAT CLUB

BETTY CONVINCES CHARLES TO INCREASE
HIS LIFE INSURANCE

"IF YOU'RE HAPPY AND YOU KNOW IT,
CLAP YOUR HANDS"

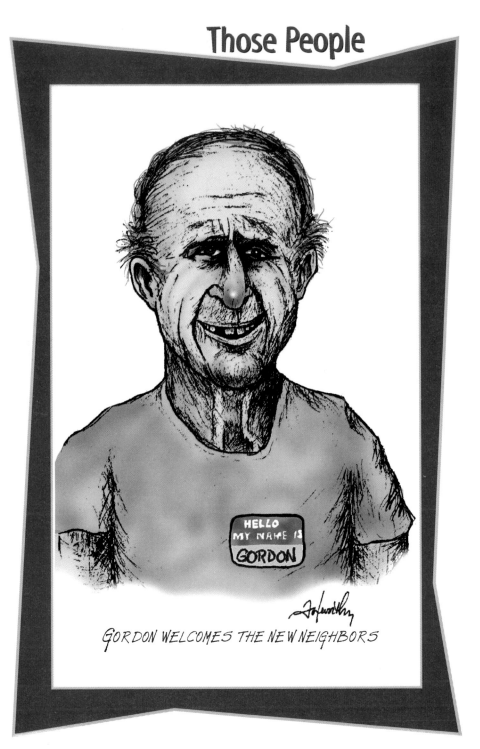

GORDON WELCOMES THE NEW NEIGHBORS

MEE-MAW'S TWO-PIECE

*CONRAD WAS INTERESTED TO LEARN
THAT A HIGH FOREHEAD WAS THOUGHT TO BE
A SIGN OF INTELLIGENCE*

BETTY LOSES HERSELF IN A
CHECK-OUT BOY FANTASY

Those People

*HANEY REALIZES
THE EASTER BUNNY ISN'T COMING*

Those People

TODD SEES HIS GRANDMOTHER NAKED

Those People

GERALD
THE GUY WHO WANTS TO GO OUT WITH YOUR MOTHER

*FRANK DELONG'S LAST 6 A.M. MOWING —
HIS NEIGHBOR PHIL WOULD MAKE SURE OF IT*

UNCLE CARLOS HITS THE DANCE FLOOR

JEAN FELT WHAT SHE DID IN HER LIVING ROOM
WHILE HARLEN WAS AT WORK WAS HER BUSINESS

CHILI COOK-OFF LEGEND—BOBO COOPER

Those People

CLEM'S 7143RD CONSECUTIVE BAD HAIR DAY

HARRY SPENDS AN AFTERNOON CONTEMPLATING PORK AND BEANS

DAVE KNEW THE DOWNSIDE OF OWNING A GREAT DANE

NED PASSES OUT IN A HAY BALER